Letta The Littlest Pony

A WJ Ranch Critter Book Series

by Jan Schiferl

WJ RANCH PUBLISHING

Published by Schiferl's WJ Ranch
55659 892 Road, Fordyce, NE 68736

www.schiferlswjranch.com

There once was a pony named Letta
who loved to frolic and play.
She lived in a place where the grass was green
on a ranch called the WJ.

The ranch was home to many,
a dog named Riley, some cows, and a cat.

Some chickens and horses of all different colors.
Now what do you think of that?

Letta was small and tiny,
the smallest horse in the pen.
She would get so sad that everyone else
could go places that she'd never been.

Tucker spends time as a cow horse.
He works to take care of the herd.
He helps catch a calf that is sick or lost.
To think he gets bored is absurd.

Lacey, the trail horse, travels on paths that curve and wind and bend.

She sees mountains and valleys
and rivers and trees.
Her adventures just never end.

Dapples and Dinky are special.
They get all fancy for shows.

They win medals and ribbons
and trophies and such
when over big fences they go.

One day a group of children
came to visit the ranch to see

All the different animals and
how life on a ranch would be.

Letta greeted all the children.
They smiled and laughed out loud.

They petted her sweetly
and gave her hugs.
Letta felt happy and proud.

That day Letta realized
she had a purpose too.
What she did was something great
that no one else could ever do.

God made everyone different,
no two of us the same.
We are all so very special,
God knows us each by name.

God Loves You!

Just like little Letta,
we can be thankful every day.
No matter if we're big or small,
God made us just that way!

CPSIA information can be obtained
at www.ICGtesting.com
Printed in the USA
LVHW072314111220
673921LV00001B/11